W9-BRQ-927

City and Rural Celebrations

Ian Rohr

A+

Smart Apple Media
P.O. Box 3263
Mankato, MN, 56002

First published in 2010 by
MACMILLAN EDUCATION AUSTRALIA PTY LTD
15–19 Claremont St, South Yarra, Australia 3141

Visit our web site at www.macmillan.com.au or go directly to www.macmillanlibrary.com.au

Associated companies and representatives throughout the world.

Copyright © Ian Rohr 2010

Library of Congress Cataloging-in-Publication Data

Library of Congress Cataloging-in-Publication Data

Rohr, Ian.
   City and country celebrations / Ian Rohr.
      p. cm. -- (Celebrations around the world)
   Includes index.
   ISBN 978-1-59920-536-6 (library binding)
   1. Festivals--Juvenile literature. 2. City and town life--Juvenile literature. 3. Country life--Juvenile literature. I. Title.
   GT3933.R62 2011
   394.26--dc22
                              2009042141

Publisher: Carmel Heron
Managing Editor: Vanessa Lanaway
Editor: Michaela Forster
Proofreader: Kirstie Innes-Will
Designer: Kerri Wilson (cover and text)
Page layout: Pier Vido
Photo researcher: Wendy Duncan
Production Controller: Vanessa Johnson

Manufactured in China by Macmillan Production (Asia) Ltd.
Kwun Tong, Kowloon, Hong Kong
Supplier Code: CP January 2010

Acknowledgments
The author and the publisher are grateful to the following for permission to reproduce copyright material:

Cover photograph: Children on a float for the annual 'Pahiyas' harvest festival in the Philippines, © Jay Directo/AFP/Getty Images

AAP Image/Dean Lewins, 27; © A Room With Views/Alamy, 25; © Bill Brooks/Alamy, 22; © Tim Graham/Alamy, 14; © Geoff Williamson Selected/Alamy, 24; Coo-ee Picture Library, 6, 18; © Firefly Productions/Corbis Edge, 5; © Robert Holmes/Corbis, 16; © Michael S. Yamashita/Corbis, 8; © Jay Directo/AFP/Getty Images, 1, 7; © Comstock/Getty Images/, 9; © TG Stock/ Getty Images, 20; © Claudio Villa/Getty Images, 10; © William West/AFP/Getty Images, 23; © iStockphoto/Gene Chutka, 4; © iStockphoto/Jason Lugo, 21; National Geographic Image Collection/Tyrone Turner, 17; Newspix, 19; Newspix/Gregg Porteous, 11; Newspix/Melanie Russell, 26; photolibrary/Bruno Perousse, 15; Reuters/Ognen Teofilovski, 13; Reuters/Picture Media/ Angelo Morelli, 12; Royal Agricultural Winter Fair, Canada, 28, 29; © Shutterstock/Kevin Renes, 30.

While every care has been taken to trace and acknowledge copyright, the publisher tenders their apologies for any accidental infringement where copyright has proved untraceable. Where the attempt has been unsuccessful, the publisher welcomes information that would redress the situation.

Contents

When a word is printed in **bold**, you can look up its meaning in the Glossary on page 31.

Celebrations

Celebrations are events that are held on special occasions. Some are events from the past that are still celebrated. Others celebrate important times in our lives or activities, such as music.

Birthdays are special events that many people celebrate.

Some celebrations involve only a few people.
Others involve whole cities or countries.
Large celebrations take place across the world.

New Year's Eve is celebrated all around
the world with fireworks.

What Are City and Rural Celebrations?

Many celebrations take place in cities around the world. They include parades and festivals. Some cities are famous for their special celebrations.

The Moomba parade is held in the city of Melbourne in Australia.

Rural celebrations are often held in small towns. They display animals, **produce**, and farming equipment. Some rural celebrations are hundreds of years old.

Harvest celebrations take place in rural areas across the world.

City Parades

Many cities celebrate special events with a parade.
Most parades have marching bands and **floats**.
Some parades take place every year.

Decorated floats are part of many parades.

Cities sometimes hold parades to cheer on a sports team. Parades can also be held to thank people who have helped the city.

Parades are popular in the United States, especially in New York City.

Keys to the City

Some cities give people the keys to the city. This shows that the people are well liked and trusted. The keys to the city are often made from metal or wood.

The keys to the city are usually given to people at a special **ceremony**.

Some people are also given the freedom of the city. This is a very old **custom**. It is given to people who have helped the city.

The freedom of the city is sometimes given to a group of people, such as this group of athletes.

City Festivals

Many cities and towns hold festivals that celebrate activities such as films and music. Sarajevo (say *sar-ra-yay-vo*), a city in Europe, has **annual** film, theater, and music festivals.

A film festival is held every year in the European city of Sarajevo.

People from around the world visit Sarajevo's festivals. Festivals such as these let people from many different places enjoy the activities.

Children from the audience are sometimes included in the performances at theater festivals.

Carnival, Brazil

Carnival is held in Rio de Janeiro and other cities in Brazil. It begins four days before the start of **Lent** and includes street parades and parties.

Some people wear amazing costumes to Carnival street parades.

People wear costumes to the parties and parades, and celebrate by dancing. In some cities, there are **samba** competitions.

Samba groups compete as part of Carnival celebrations.

Mardi Gras, United States

Mardi Gras is a celebration held in New Orleans, Louisiana. It takes place in the weeks before Lent. There are parades every day.

There is usually a big parade each day of Mardi Gras.

The parades and parties are organized by **krewes**. Different krewes parade in different parts of the city. They throw toys and presents into the crowd.

Krewes parade on decorated floats during Mardi Gras.

Anniversary Celebrations

Many cities and country towns celebrate the year they were **founded**. These are called anniversaries. Special celebrations are usually held when a place reaches a **centennial**.

In 2001, the centennial of the Australian nation was celebrated around the country.

Schools often celebrate the year they began.
They hold special events to celebrate their history
and success. Older students often return to the
school for these celebrations.

Schools usually hold special events and activities
to celebrate anniversaries.

Country Fairs

Many country towns hold an annual fair where farmers display their best animals and produce. There are also competitions for the best cakes, jams, sewing, and artworks.

Farmers display their animals at country fairs.

In country towns the fair is often the highlight of the year. People come from all around the area. There are activities such as dancing and choosing a fair queen.

Fun rides are popular at country fairs.

Rodeos

Rodeos celebrate people who work with horses and cattle. They are popular in the United States, Canada, and Australia.

The Calgary Stampede in Canada is one of the largest rodeos in the world.

Rodeo events include horseback riding, bull riding, and calf roping. Riders compete to stay on a **bucking** animal the longest. Rodeo clowns entertain the crowd and also help the riders.

The rodeo clowns lead the bulls away from falling riders.

Gymkhanas

Gymkhanas (say *jim-kar-nas*) are festivals usually held in country towns. They are often organized by pony clubs and include show jumping competitions and races.

Show jumping events are popular at gymkhanas.

There are many children's events at gymkhanas.
There are also fun events such as fancy dress
for horses and riders.

Competitors try to get their horses and outfits
looking as neat as they can.

Sydney Royal Easter Show,
Australia

The Sydney Royal Easter Show started in 1823.
The show is held for two weeks over Easter.
It includes many animal and produce displays
from the country.

Wood chopping
is a popular event
at the Sydney Royal
Easter Show.

There are competitions for the best animals, wool, vegetables, and other produce. The show also has many fun rides and stalls.

The grand parade of farm animals is one of the show's highlights.

Royal Agricultural Winter Fair, Canada

The Royal **Agricultural** Winter Fair is held for two weeks in November. It is held in Toronto, Canada. The Fair is nearly 100 years old.

Horses and their riders perform at the Royal Agricultural Winter Fair.

Visitors can see rodeos, horse shows, and dog shows. Farmers display their crops and animals and learn about new equipment.

Farmers display the large vegetables they have grown.

Try This!

Find the answers to these questions in the book.
(You can check your answers on page 32.)

1 Where is the Royal Agricultural Winter Fair held?

2 What do rodeos celebrate?

3 When was the Sydney Royal Easter Show first held?

4 How do people celebrate Carnival in Brazil?

5 Which European city has film, theater, and music festivals?

Try This Activity

Next time you celebrate a special occasion with your friends or family, ask yourself:

- Why are you celebrating?

- How long have people been celebrating this event?

- Are there other places in the world where people celebrate the event?

30

Glossary

agricultural   related to farming, such as growing plants or keeping animals

annual   happens every year

bucking   jumping and kicking to throw off a rider

centennial   the celebration of 100 years

ceremony   an activity that is performed on a special occasion

custom   a belief or activity that has been passed from older people to younger people

floats   vehicles decorated for a parade

founded   first built or started

harvest   when the fruits and vegetables on farms are gathered or picked

krewes   groups that organize parades

Lent   the 40 days that lead up to Easter

produce   the fruit and vegetables grown on a farm

rodeos   events that feature cattle roping, bull riding, and horseback riding

samba   a type of Brazilian dance

Index

Answers to the Quiz on Page 30

1 Canada
2 People who work with horses and cattle
3 1823
4 With street parades and parties
5 Sarajevo